# JERUSALEM
# THE HOLY

# JERUSALEM THE HOLY

PROF. MICHAEL AVI-YONAH

PHOTOGRAPHY   WERNER BRAUN

SCHOCKEN BOOKS · NEW YORK

# CONTRIBUTORS

## Prof. Michael Avi-Yonah

Professor of Archaeology
and History of Art,
Hebrew University of Jerusalem

Captions and Chronology
## Louis Williams

Chief Photographer
## Werner Braun

Design
Yishai Afek

Printed in Israel

© SADAN Publishing House Ltd..
P.O.B. 16096 Tel-Aviv, Israel

First published by **SCHOCKEN BOOKS** 1976
**Library of Congress Cataloging in Publication Data**
Avi-Yonah, Michael, 1904–1974
  Jerusalem the Holy.
  1. Jerusalem—Description—Views. I. Braun, Werner;
1912–    II. Title.
DS109.2.A953    1976    956.94`4    75–24510
ISBN 0-8052-3604-X

Jacket illustration
The Heavenly Jerusalem

back cover
The Walls and the Gates
of the Old City

Title Page
Jerusalem at sunset

Endpapers
Messiah at the Gates of
Jerusalem—A woodcut
Illustration from the Passover
Haggadah (Venice, 1629)

# JERUSALEM THE HOLY

## A Short History
## by Prof. Michael Avi-Yonah

"THE HOLY CITY", "YERUSHALAYIM HA-QEDOSHA" (HEBREW), AND "AL-QUDS" (Arabic) are three different expressions of religious exaltation which are applied to a rather provincial city of middling size, situated on a hilly ridge some distance away from the sea and from the great international trade routes. And yet time and again this city has served as the focus of tremendous historical and religious forces, a symbol of heavenly bliss on earth and a magnet which through the centuries has drawn millions of pilgrims. In varying degrees of intensity, it is a religious symbol for about half the human race: 980 million Christians, 475 million Moslems and 13 million Jews.

The city's geographical and topographical position cannot in itself explain this phenomenon, although we can say at least that these elements, as well as the climate and other natural conditions, do not preclude its religious function. In a certain sense Jerusalem's physical handicaps have proven blessings in disguise. It was far from the two great international trade routes crossing Palestine in antiquity—the Sea Road and the King's Highway from Damascus to the Red Sea. On the other hand, the city is located near the less important Watershed Road which bisects the mountains of Ephraim and Judah from north to south. Access from the west is via several not-especially-difficult passes; from the east it is less easy but still feasible. The city had barely enough land and water for its own needs, but human ingenuity supplied what was necessary to sustain all its visitors. It stands very near to the dividing line between desert land and that which is cultivated, enabling anyone disgusted with the bustle and iniquity of society to find refuge in the Judean desert, which stretches eastwards as far as the Jordan River. The city's area itself is sliced up by many small valleys into scores of hills which in earliest times made possible a pluralistic religious life with no more than a tolerable amount of interfaith strife.

3

## "THE FOUNDATION OF THE GOD SHALEM"

In one sense the city was a religious foundation from the very beginning. Its very name attests to this: it means "the Foundation of the (god) Shalem". Shalem was a western Semitic deity the root of whose name is identical with the words meaning "completeness" and "peace". Melchizedek, king of *Salem* (almost certainly *Jerusalem*, third millennium BCE) was "priest of God Most High" (in Hebrew, *El Elyon*, the name of an important Canaanite deity) (Genesis 14:18). The second half of his name, which means "justice", reappears in the name of Adonizedek king of Jerusalem who led five Amorite kings against Joshua (Joshua 10:1). Still, we should not attach too much importance to these manifestations of Canaanite religiosity in connection with Jerusalem, because as far as we can tell, every Canaanite city was supposed to be the property of one or another god or *ba'al* (meaning "owner"), for whom the king on earth acted as viceroy. This is connected with the Canaanite cities' sacral origin, their nucleus usually being a temple.

In contemplating Jerusalem's religious history as reflected in the chronicles and teaching of the three great monotheistic religions, we have many different aspects to consider: the historical evolution, the scriptural texts and their later formulations in theological literature, the forecast of Jerusalem's role in the eschatology, and the city's religious reality as it has evolved through the centuries. Finally, we may attempt to estimate the amount of importance that each religion accords Jerusalem, in so far as such metaphysical matters can be defined and estimated.

The demise of Canaanism has left Judaism as the faith whose roots in Jerusalem go furthest into the past. Yet the city is not mentioned by name in the Pentateuch (the case of "Salem" excepted) but is merely referred to as "the place the Lord thy God shall choose to put His name there" (Deut. 12:21). However at no time during the Israelite tribes' period of settlement

4

was the amphictyonic sanctuary at Shiloh ever regarded as something permanent; it still reflected the conditions of the desert wandering in which the Ark of the Covenant had no fixed abode.

CITY OF DAVID

It is fitting that the historical personage who linked Jerusalem for all time with the history of Judaism was David, the legendary hero, the "servant of the Lord" and ancestor of the Messiah to come. He took Jerusalem, then the City of the Jebusites, and made it the capital of his kingdom. He also brought the Ark of the Covenant there, setting it up provisionally on the "threshing floor" of Aravnah, the last Jebusite king, after purchasing the land from its owner. David set up an altar on the spot "and offered burnt offerings and peace offerings" (2 Sam. 24:25). In a sense the spiritual essence of a sanctuary was already present and all that was left for David's son Solomon to do was to clothe it in an architectural reality. "And the word of the Lord came to Solomon... I will dwell among the Children of Israel" (I Kings 6:11–13). As Solomon himself said in his dedicatory prayer: "I have built thee an exalted house, a place for thee to dwell forever" (I Kings 8:13).

THE CITY OF GOD

During the first centuries of its existence, the uniqueness of the Temple and of Jerusalem its abode was by no means generally recognized. In Israel, Jeroboam built rival sanctuaries at Dan and Bethel, and even in Judah the excavations of Lachish and Arad have shown that from the time of Solomon to that of Josiah, sanctuaries of the God of Israel existed also in other places. Nevertheless, as the external dangers grew, threatening to inundate Jerusalem's image the "House of the Lord" began to glow with a supranatural aura. As Isaiah said in the face of the apparently irresistible onslaught

5

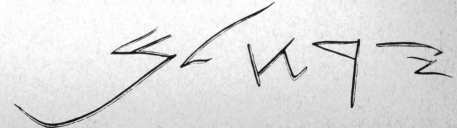

of Sennacherib of Assyria, "I will defend this city to save it, for my sake and for the sake of my servant David" (2 Kings 19:34). The reforms of Josiah meant the end of the "high places" with which the local temples were now identified, and the cult's concentration in Jerusalem and Jerusalem alone. The great prophets of Judah were not blind to the sins of Jerusalem as an earthly city and they fiercely denounced them, but at the same time they foresaw a splendid future for the city after it had been "purified": "For out of Zion shall go forth the law and the word of the Lord from Jerusalem" (Isaiah 2:3). When the doom they had prophesied came to pass and the majority of the people found itself in exile by the waters of Babylon, their love of Jerusalem found expression in the words of Psalm 137, which have echoed down through the centuries: "If I forget you, Jerusalem, let my right hand wither!" (Psalm 137:5). After depicting Jerusalem's abasement in the crudest terms, the prophet Ezekiel devoted the last chapters of his book to a vision of the city and Temple restored in which the future Jerusalem is outlined in the greatest detail.

After the first return to Zion Jerusalem's position in Judaism became completely unassailable. Though the Second Temple was much more modest at the beginning than the First, it had no competitor for many centuries. The Temple and the City remained the focus of a Jewish national life now spreading through a rapidly-growing Diaspora. The ascendancy of the Halachic way of life in the Persian and later periods meant a greater frequency of pilgrimages to Jerusalem, on the three holidays especially designated for this purpose. Nor did the pilgrims come empty-handed. We need only mention the "Nicanor who made the gates" as he is referred to in an ossuary inscription; his case is simply better documented than many others. A rich Jew of Alexandria, Nicanor had gates prepared for the portal which separated the two courts of the Inner Temple. He and his gates miraculously escaped the perils of the sea, and the beauty of their bronze was such that it was

decided to leave them without the gilding common to all the other gates of the Temple.

Jerusalem's dominant role in Jewish life in the last centuries before the Second Temple's destruction is also attested to by the Acts of the Apostles (2:5–11). Herod devoted a large part of his resources to rebuilding the Temple with such magnificence that even the rabbis, who by no means approved of him, had to admit that "He who never saw Herod's temple has never seen a magnificent structure". When the Zealots rose up against Rome, their shekels were minted with the legend "Jerusalem the Holy". In the Second Revolt (or the war of Bar Kokhba) the city's restoration to the Jews was commemorated on coins and was regarded as the revolt's greatest achievement.

## AELIA CAPITOLINA

The disasters of the two revolts and the transformation of Jerusalem into a Roman provincial city named Aelia Capitolina did not in any way dampen the ardour of Jewish devotion. The Temple's measurements and other religious regulations concerning Jerusalem were recorded with meticulous care for the Restoration which was certain to come. Though the Jews were forbidden by law to enter Jerusalem, pilgrimages were resumed the first moment Roman vigilance relaxed. In the third century they became so common in fact that a leading rabbi was able to remark: "Anyone who wishes to go up to Jerusalem, may do so".

In the following centuries, Jews were sometimes allowed to settle in Jerusalem, while at other times they were expelled or even massacred. Yet their devotion to the city did not and could not change. The black patch which stood on the walls of many houses in the Diaspora as a memento of the temple and holy city was only one of the many marks of this longing. With the rise of

European influence in the Turkish Empire in the nineteenth and twentieth centuries, the number of Jews who found it possible to live in Jerusalem steadily increased. In fact, starting in the second half of the nineteenth century the city had a Jewish majority, although it took many long years for this demographic fact to find municipal expression. In 1948–49 the whole course of Israel's War of Independence was influenced by the firm resolution of the Jews to retain at least part of Jerusalem. Now that the Six Day War of 1967 has restored Jewish rule to the old (Holy) City, the confrontation between the mundane city and its religious image and between the Jewish Jerusalem and that of the other two religions, for which it is holy, may be said to have only just begun.

JESUS IN JERUSALEM

In contrast to the Jewish attitude towards Jerusalem which is based on thousands of years of history and an entire galaxy of heroes and prophets, Christian Jerusalem bears the imprint of one great event: the expiatory death on the Cross, the Resurrection and Ascension. Of course, early Christianity's connection with Jerusalem is not limited merely to the story of the Passion. According to the Gospels (Luke 2:22) Jesus as an infant was presented at the Temple, and as a boy of twelve he amazed the rabbis there with his understanding (Luke 2:46–47). Yet it was in the final days that most of the Christian events in Jerusalem took place: the triumphant entry, the prophecy about the destruction of the Temple (Mark 13:2), the miracle at the pool of Bethesda (John 5:2), the Last Supper, Gethsemane, the house of Caiaphas, the palace of Herod Antipas, the praetorium of Pilate, the Way of the Cross, the Crucifixion, the burial, the Resurrection and finally the Ascension. In the Christian tradition the sites of all these events have been precisely located. Although the central site, that of the Resurrection, was built over in Roman times by a Temple of Venus that adjoined the forum of Aelia Capitolina, Christian sources maintain that its location was handed

down from one bishop to another until the time of the Emperor Constantine and his mother Helena in the fourth century. It was through the efforts of Constantine and his successors that Byzantine Jerusalem became a Christian city. They built the magnificent Church of the Resurrection (335) and that of Helena on the Mount of Olives. The Madaba mosaic map shows a town full of churches, monasteries, hospices for pilgrims and for the aged and infirm etc. Though it had its share of the troubles that divided Christian-dom in that period, the Holy City was always highly regarded. Its elevation to a Patriarchate equal in rank to those of Constantinople, Antioch and Alexandria was but one sign of this esteem. The fact that it served as a city of refuge for people who had fallen out of favour in court and for the relatives of fallen ministers and Emperors, further added to its air of sanctity. A third factor was the presence in the City and its environs of a number of Christian refugees from the barbarians who had devastated Italy. These members of the Roman aristocracy did much to enhance the city's Christian character. Some of its leaders such as Cyril of Jerusalem influenced Christian thought. The splendours of Byzantine Jerusalem were tarnished by the Persian invasion of 614, and in 638 the City fell to the Moslems. During the first centuries of Arab rule the Christian community remained unmolested, and as "People of the Book" they were exempt from payment of a poll tax. Yet from the ninth century onwards, as tension in the Moslem world increased, the situation of the Christian minority deteriorated. Pilgrims were molested, extortion was rampant and not even the Church of the Holy Sepulchre was immune to the vandalism of the Caliph Hakim (966–1021).

The Christian response was the Crusades and for one century the Holy City was again under Christian rule. The Europeans' tremendous energy left its mark upon the City's churches, beginning with the Church of the Holy Sepulchre, though the occupation of the Patriarchal See by a Latin bishop added fuel to the latent conflict between the Catholic and the Greek Orthodox churches. The rift continued under the rule of the Mamelukes

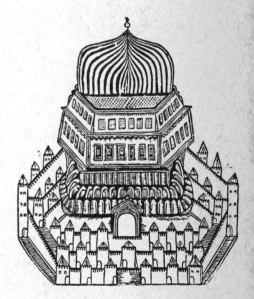

9

and Turks after the Moslem reconquest. The Franciscan fathers of the Custodia di Terra Santa continued their lonely vigil on behalf of Catholic interests, but for a long time, and in particular after the Ottoman conquest in 1517, the Greek Orthodox had the upper hand. It was they who rebuilt the Holy Sepulchre after the fire of 1808, and who set up an iconostasis in the Crusader ambulatory.

Latin Christianity began to revive in Jerusalem in the nineteenth century as European powers made their weight felt in the Levant. The restoration of the Latin Patriarchade in 1846 and the establishment of a Protestant bishopric were two milestones in this process. The British Mandate, though formally a period of Christian rule, left little trace upon the city's Christian life. On the other hand, the ecumenic trend of recent decades has led to a degree of co-operation between the various churches which a generation ago would have seemed utopian. While the establishment of Christian institutes of learning has contributed greatly to the community's spiritual revival.

MOHAMMED IN JERUSALEM

The third religious entity that has standing in Jerusalem is of course Islam. Although political control of the city was in non-Moslem hands for only 138 years during the last thirteen centuries, the third monotheistic religion was late in developing a "special relationship" to it. And when it did it was largely motivated by external events such as the challenge by non-Islamic forces, and Jerusalem was never allowed the status of the two senior Islamic cities, Mecca and Medina. There was only a short period of eighteen years during which by order of the Prophet, Moslems prayed facing Jerusalem, probably to lure prospective Jewish converts. When this did not succeed, the *qibla* (direction of prayer) was changed to Mecca. Although Jerusalem was in Moslem hands from 638 onwards they claimed only a modest praying place at the south end of the Temple esplanade. It was the Umayyad Caliph

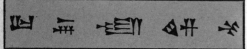

10

Abd el Malik (685–705) who first decided to make Jerusalem a counter-weight to Mecca on the one hand (the Hejaz was for a decade in the hands of the anti-Caliph Abdallah ibn Zubayr) and the Byzantine Christians on the other. It was he who ordered the erection of the Dome of the Rock, the oldest Moslem sanctuary still standing, and one of the most beautiful.

Consecrated in 691, it was meant to outshine the dome of the Resurrection (Church of the Holy Sepulchre) and serve as a focus for pilgrimage. In the latter aim it did not succeed, and in any case Mecca soon returned to Umayyad rule. The Moslems however now developed a new interpretation for sura 17:1 in the Koran which reads "Praise be to Him who transported his servant by night from the Sacred Mosque (Mecca) to the Furthermost Mosque, the precinct of which we have blessed." Originally meant to describe Mohammed's ride to heaven, it now referred to a nocturnal ride on the legendary steed al-Buraq to the Jerusalem Mosque now known as al-Aqsa ("The Furthest"). This new interpretation and efforts to augment Jerusalem's sanctity under the influence of Jewish converts to Islam, aroused opposition from the more conservative teachers of the faith. Another stimulus was needed for Jerusalem's sanctity to be enhanced in Moslem eyes, and again it was an external one. The Crusades made the possession of the Holy City an object of contention between Christians and Moslems. The ultimate Moslem victory under Saladin was received with rejoicing throughout the Moslem world, which was now suddenly conscious of what it had lost and regained. "The Ka'aba (in Mecca) rejoiced in the redemption of its brother al-Aqsa". Under the Mamelukes, a determined effort was made to Islamise the Holy City as far as possible. Once again it served as a place of refuge or semi-banishment for emirs in disgrace, who used their wealth to endow and establish a ring of Moslem *madrasas* (houses of study), *zawiyas* (monasteries) and *turbes* (mausoleums) around the Temple esplanade. This part of Jerusalem has retained its Moslem character from that time down to the present.

## A HEAVENLY JERUSALEM

From the days of the Prophets down to the present, the religious-minded visitor to Jerusalem has been struck by the contrast between its metaphysical sanctity and a mundane day to day life which sometimes degenerates to outright squalor. To the mystically inclined, two possible solutions, not mutually exclusive, have for centuries presented themselves. One is that Jerusalem the downtrodden shall rise to its true splendour at some future time, the other is that there already exists another city, a Heavenly Jerusalem, which at some future time shall descend to earth or at least serve as the prototype for the true Jerusalem. Each of the three religions has interpreted the concept of a heavenly and eschatological Jerusalem in its own way, depending on the ultimate view it holds of the city's sanctity. For the Jews, the Divine Presence *(Shekhina)* has always been inherent in the conception of Jerusalem. Up to the time of the Destruction, its focal point was naturally in the Temple, but even after that it was supposed never to budge from the Western (or Wailing) Wall; this was expressed as early as the fourth century by Rabbi Aha (Midrash Exodus Rabba 2:2). The Jewish conception of the Messianic period is not of a descent upon earth of the heavenly Jerusalem but rather a restoration of the Davidic Dynasty in all its glory in a City and Temple that have been rebuilt and purified. In this view, Jerusalem also occupies a prominent position as the capital of the Land of Israel, a position which it enjoyed in actual fact only under Jewish rule. It has and always will be a place of human habitation, striving insofar as possible to reproduce the holiness of the Heavenly City on earth. The peace and justice which will reign in Messianic time will be the result of the extension of a vision of Jerusalem throughout the world.

The Christian conception of Jerusalem differs from the Jewish one in that it is entirely oriented towards a single future event — the Second Coming of Christ. Though this event may be connected with the Mount of Olives from which, according to tradition, Jesus ascended to heaven, in significance it is universal rather than local. And the medieval conception of the Last Judgement and General Resurrection in the Valley of Jehoshaphat between the city and the Mount of Olives, though picturesque, is hardly a dogma. Christian mysticism tends rather to concentrate on the "Jerusalem above which is free" (St. Paul to the Galatians 4:25). In Revelations (21:1–2) the "New heaven and new earth" shall come, "And I saw the holy city, new Jerusalem, coming down out of heaven from God prepared as a bride adorned for her husband". Presumably the old city had passed away with the old earth.

Moslem tradition gives Jerusalem (or rather the al-Aqsa Mosque) third place in importance. "There is no nobler purpose than a visit to the three mosques: the mosque of Mecca, my own mosque (that of Medina) and the mosque of Jerusalem" (al-Aqsa) is a tradition attributed to Mohammed himself. Instead of a heavenly Jerusalem it is the Ka'aba of Mecca which will ultimately, "like a bride", be transferred to Jerusalem together with all the pilgrims. On the Day of Judgement, humanity will be made to pass by the angel Asrafil over a bridge as narrow as a razor stretching from the Mount of Olives to the Temple Mount. Only the just will get through, the evil will fall down into the pit of Gehennom *(Ge Bene Hinnom = the Valley of the Sons of Hinnom, the biblical name of one of the valleys that encircle Jerusalem on the west and the south).

The mystical conception of Jerusalem's role in the future was a projection of its sanctity in the present. In Jewish sources the Holy City is holier than the rest of the Holy Land and thus holier than the rest of the world by two degrees. It contains the Temple, in which there are seven more degrees of holiness culminating the Holy of Holies.

The Christian idea of Jerusalem's holiness has two origins: one, the fact that

the mystery of Transubstantiation and of the Redemption and the Resurrection took place on its soil; the other the fact that the Church Fathers beginning with St. Paul regarded Christianity as the rightful successor of Israel in the biblical sense. Thus, all the prophecies and promises were transferred from the people of the Old to that of the New Testament including of course the special holiness of Jerusalem, as expressed among others by Ezekiel: "This is Jerusalem; I have set her in the midst of the nations" (5:5). The city's spiritual aspect was naturally emphasized still further after the failure of the Crusades.

The Moslem attitude to Jerusalem was influenced by both Jewish and Christian traditions. According to one source: "Twenty thousand angels intervened before God for every inhabitant of Jerusalem".

PILGRIMAGE TO JERUSALEM

The superior holiness of Jerusalem attracted two kinds of people: those who came to sanctify themselves at the holy sites and then return home — the pilgrims — and those who decided to spend the rest of their lives there in contemplation of infinity — the mystics. Around these two trends there crystallized an entire establishment, also on two levels: an ecclesiastical hierarchy to take care of the spiritual needs, and a mundane infrastructure to take care of physical needs.

Pilgrimage to Jerusalem by Jews was only interrupted with the City's destruction and for all practical purposes never ceased. We find scattered references to it in the Talmudic sources often embroidered with legendary elements such as the story of Rabbi Jose ben Halafta who met the Prophet Elijah there and heard the *Shekhina* weeping over the ruins. Even in Byzantine times, when the old Roman edicts forbidding Jews to visit Jerusalem was strictly enforced, an exception was made for the pilgrimage of the Ninth of

14

Av, when Jews were wont to lament and to anoint the "Pierced Stone" (probably the rock over which the Dome of the Rock now stands).

Christian pilgrimages began in the second century and continued to grow through the ages. Even in the worst periods—the seventeenth and eighteenth centuries when Europe was first devastated by war then dominated by Rationalism—there were always groups of pilgrims who came to visit the Holy Sites. A vast literature of "itineraria" or descriptions of the Holy Land grew up through the centuries, some of them only a few pages long, others in many volumes. Moslems who came to perform the "meritorious deed" *(ziyara)* of a visit to the al-Aqsa have been recorded from the entire world of Islam, from Morocco to Persia and India.

If a mere visit to the Holy City was regarded as bestowing divine grace or freedom from sin, this applied *a fortiori* to dwelling there. Jewish mysticism—the Kaballah—was centred on Jerusalem from the very beginning. In the past, however circumstances for its growth there were not favourable and it was Safed which became pre-eminently the city of the old Kabbalists. On the other hand, Hassidic mysticism, with its greater practicality, managed to strike roots in Jerusalem. Since the year 1702, when Rabbi Judah "the Hassid" of Siedlec, Poland, redeemed the Hurvah Synagogue, the city has never lacked its mystics. The Hassidic communities of the Rabbis of Gur, Lubavich and Szatmar may differ in their attitude to the State of Israel and modern Jerusalem, but they all add to the city's picturesque character. The religious quarters, centred upon Meah Shearim, the oldest, have a peculiar flavour which is greatly appreciated by visitors. Especially on Sabbaths and holidays, their residents' fur hats and bright velvet coats form a remarkable sight. With the city's re-unification in 1967 and the return of the Wailing Wall to Jewish hands, the Old City and in particular the praying area in front of the wall have become a centre of activity for Hassidim ranging from Habad intellectuals to modern mystics of the type fashioned among today's youth. Jewish orthodoxy in the city is represented by hundreds of synagogues and there is even the modest beginning of a Reform movement. The traditional *yeshivot* where Talmudic law is still taught by the methods of centuries ago stand side by side with modern centres of Talmudic learning where computers are an accepted tool of the scholar.

Jerusalem's Christian community is even more variegated than the Jewish one and reflects every facet of the Christian world. There are the traditional ecclesiastical authorities such as the Greek Orthodox Patriarchate (in Arabic, *Deir el Rum* of "House of Rome" recalling the fact that this institution inherited the Byzantine (East Roman) Empire); then there are the Catholic Patriarchate, a relatively modern institution but allied with the Franciscan Custodia di Terra Santa; the Armenian Patriarchate, and the heads of the Greek Uniate, Armenian Uniate, Coptic and Abyssinian churches—the list is by no means complete. The protestant communities are represented by the Anglican bishopric of St. George, a German pastorate, and numerous other groups among which the Baptists are among the most numerous. The city's Christian aspect is enhanced by its learned institutions, mostly founded by monastic orders, but some of them secular: the Dominican *Ecole biblique et archéologique française*, the Franciscan *Studium biblicum*, the Benedictines on Mount Zion, and the American, British and German schools of archaeology.

THE ETERNAL CITY

We may try, in conclusion, to assess Jerusalem's impact on each of the three religions for which it is *the* or *a* Holy City.

For Moslems, Jerusalem's holiness is bound up with the historical domination of a proud and universalist faith which is marked by a profound submission to the Divine Will.

Judaism, by its very nature a national-universalist religion, is and always has been focused on the Holy City. Its holidays, its prayers and a good deal of its religious legislation become meaningless without reference to this central point, the "navel of the universe" as the *Aggadah* has it. The problem of secular vs. religious Jerusalem, which confronts the State of Israel by no means detracts from the Holy City's intrinsic importance, on which all Jews are agreed.

Christianity is a universal religion free from the trammels of nationality, whose beginnings were marked by a historical event localized in space and time in and around Jerusalem. Though the city's importance in Christian eyes has varied from time to time and varies along the spectrum of ecumenic Christianity, the spiritual elevation connected with the luminous character of the Holy Sites is now generally accepted. Because of its universal and transcendental character, the Christian presence in Jerusalem required less material content than other faiths.

Prof. Michael Avi-Yonah

# 4000 YEARS OF HISTORY

| | | |
|---|---|---|
| *Canaanite Period* *—1000 B.C.E.* | | Earliest archaeological evidence of settlement. First written records of Jerusalem, the Egyptian *Execration Texts,* indicate the city as Canaanite. |
| | 18th Century | Melchi-zedek, King of Salem welcomes Abraham, with 'bread and wine'. |
| | 1250 | Joshua defeats the king of Jerusalem, head of the alliance of cities, but the city remains Jebusite. |
| *Israelite Period* *1000–587* | 1000 | David defeats the Jebusites, and moves his capital to Jerusalem from Hebron. |
| | 961 | Solomon begins construction of the 1st Temple and the city walls. |
| | 928 | Shishak of Egypt sacks the city. |
| | 922 | The United Kingdom divides into Israel and Judah. |
| | 715 | Hezekiah, King of Judah, rules over Jerusalem and constructs the Water Tunnel and Siloam Pool to safeguard the city's source of water. |
| | 701 | Sennacherib, King of Assyria, lays siege to Jerusalem, but is repelled. |
| | 587 | Nebuchadnezzar takes the city, destroys the Temple and exiles the Jews to Babylon. |
| *Persian Period* *537–332* | 537 | The return from Babylon begins, in the reign of Cyrus. Construction of the 2nd Temple is begun under Sheshbazzar, Governor of Judah, and is continued by his nephew, Zerubbabel. |

18

| | | |
|---|---|---|
| | 515 | In the reign of Darius, the 2nd Temple is completed. |
| | 445 | Nehemiah (is sent as Governor, by Artaxerxes-I, and) completes the fortifications of Jerusalem. |
| | 332 | Alexander the Great of Macedon conquers the Persian Empire, but leaves Jerusalem untouched. |
| *Hellenistic Period 332–167* | 312 | After a series of battles between Alexander's generals, Ptolemy wins control over Jerusalem, and takes Jewish prisoners to Alexandria. |
| | 312–198 | Rule of the Ptolemaic dynasty. Ptolemy II inaugurates the translation of the Bible into Greek, bringing Jewish scholars from Jerusalem to Alexandria for the purpose. |
| | 198 | Antiochus III drives the Egyptians from the city. |
| | 198–167 | The Seleucids rule Jerusalem. |
| | 169 | Antiochus Epiphanes sacks the city and plunders the Temple. |
| *Hasmonean Period 167–63* | 164 | The Maccabees reconquer the city and rededicate the Temple. |
| | 63 | Pompey occupies Jerusalem. |
| *Roman Period 63 B.C.E.– 324 C.E.* | 40 | The Romans are driven out and the city briefly ruled by Mattathias Antigonus, the Hasmonean King. |
| | 37– 4 | Reign of Herod the Great, who builds the Antonina Fortress and starts to rebuild the Temple. |

| | | |
|---|---|---|
| 26 C.E. | | Pontius Pilate is appointed Procurator of Judea. |
| 33 | | Jesus is crucified in Jerusalem. |
| 41 | | Agrippa, King of Judea and grandson of Herod, builds the Third Wall of the City. |
| 66 | | The Jews revolt against Roman oppression. The Great Revolt culminates in the fall of Jerusalem and destruction of the 2nd Temple by Titus (70). |
| 132 | | The Jews, led by Bar Kochba, drive out the Romans and again make Jerusalem the Jewish Capital. |
| 135 | | The Emperor Hadrian destroys Jerusalem and builds a new walled city —Aelia Capitolina, with a temple dedicated to Jupiter on Mount Moriah. |
| 136 | | The City, under Roman rule, enjoys perhaps the quietest period in its history, as a sleepy provincial town, forbidden to Jews, but visited by Christian pilgrims. |
| *Byzantine Period 324–638* | 324 | Constantine of Byzantium conquers Jerusalem, thereby inaugurating the first Christian rule over the city. |
| | 326 | Helena, mother of Constantine, visits Jerusalem at the instigation of Bishop Macarius of Aelia Capitolina, and identifies the sites connected with Jesus, causing churches to be built on them. |

20

| | | |
|---|---|---|
| | 336 | Constantine builds the Church of the Holy Sepulchre. |
| | 361 | Julianus permits the Jews to return, and preparations are made for reconstruction of the Temple. |
| | 614 | Chosroes II, Emperor of Persia, lays siege to Jerusalem, helped by the Jews of Galilee, and after 20 days occupies the City, sending thousands of Christians and the True Cross to Persia. |
| | 629 | The Byzantine Emperor, Heraclius, returns to Jerusalem and massacres the Jews, expelling the survivors. |
| *Moslem Period* *638–1099* | 638 | The City capitulates to Omar, the 2nd Moslem Caliph, who erects the first wooden mosque on Harem esh-Sharif—Mount Moriah. The Jews return to Jerusalem. |
| | 691 | The Dome of the Rock, so-called Mosque of Omar, is completed by the Umayyad Caliph, Abd el-Malik. |
| | 1016 | A severe earthquake damages the Dome of the Rock, which is repaired 6 years later. |
| *Crusader Kingdom* *1099–1187* | 1099 | The Crusaders led by Godfrey de Bouillon conquer Jerusalem. De Bouillon becomes the 'Defender of the Holy Sepulchre'. |
| | 1100 | Godfrey's brother, Baldwin, is enthroned as the 1st Crusader King of a Jerusalem, where Moslems and Jews are forbidden to reside. |

21

| | 1187 | Jerusalem returns to Islam after conquest by Saladin, who restores Moslem and Jewish inhabitation of the City. |
| | 1229 | Frederick II of Germany, Holy Roman Emperor, enters into alliance with Sultan al-Kamil of Egypt, and is ceded Jerusalem, while the Moslems retain control of Harem esh-Sharif. |
| *Mameluke Period* *1250–1517* | 1260 | The city is pillaged by the Tartars. |
| | 1267 | The Mamelukes take control of Jerusalem and inaugurate a period of architectural beautification of Moslem Jerusalem. They also rebuild the walls of the city. |
| | 1400 | The City is sacked by Genghis Khan's Mongols. |
| *Ottoman Turkish Period 1517–1917* | 1517 | Salim I conquers Jerusalem. |
| | 1538 | Suleiman the Magnificent rebuilds the City ramparts, in their present form. |
| | 1860 | The first Jewish suburbs are built outside the walls. |
| | 1869 | The road from the coast to Jerusalem is completed. |
| *British Mandatory Period 1917–1948* | 1917 | General Allenby enters Jerusalem, at the head of a British army. |
| | 1948 | Arab-Jewish War. The State of Israel is proclaimed with Jerusalem as its capital—a divided city. |
| | 1967 | The Six-Day War reunites the City and reopens all the holy shrines to all comers. |

# THE ILLUSTRATIONS

An inspiring view of ancient Jerusalem. The golden Dome of the Rock, emblem of the city, stands on the peak of Mount Moriah, revered by Jews as the site of the *Holy of Holies,* at the heart of the First and Second Temples; by Moslems as the *Harem esh-Sharif,* third holiest shrine in Islam, from whence Muhammad began his fabled night ascent to Heaven—and by Christians as the place consecrated by the Crusaders as *Templum Domini,* at the heart of the City so involved in Jesus' life and death. This plaza, a meeting place for the emotions and concepts of the three great monotheistic religions, is the legendary place where Abraham offered up Isaac in sacrifice. It has trembled under the mailed feet of almost every great empire and army in the history of mankind: some came to loot and pillage, others to impose their religions and cultures, and yet others to seek the prestige that possession of this City could grant, since the beginnings of faith in the One God of the patriarch Abraham.

1

*"As the mountains are round Jerusalem . . ."*
The westward hills (*L*) of Jerusalem face into the sea winds and enjoy plentiful rain. Forests flourish and people live. To the east (*R*), steep arid slopes fall towards the Judean Desert and the searing Jordan Valley. Olives and vineyards cling stubbornly to the valley bottoms to gain what benefit they can from the soil, eroded from the upper slopes and the low water table of sparse rainfall.

The two and a half mile long wall of the Old City, completed in its present form by Suleiman the Magnificent (1539), through four millenia, kept in—and held out—a long succession of men who have made their mark in the annals of mankind. Emperors, warriors and kings who changed the map of the world. Prophets and priests who sought to inspire men's thoughts. Travellers and pilgrims from afar, who journeyed to worship and seek their roots. The Damascus—or Nablus Gate (*above*), most ornate of the City's seven gates, was, until the 19th century, the gate through which foreign dignitaries entered the city. That honour was later transferred to the Jaffa—or el-Halil Gate (*R*).

A panoramic view of the walled city, with the City of David in the right foreground. His city— *the stronghold of Zion*—that he took from the Jebusites, by capturing the water sources of the Kidron Valley, is believed to have extended along the Ophel Ridge to the south of Moriah, where his son Solomon would later build the great First Temple. The work of Dr. Kathleen Kenyon, the famed archaeologist, has confirmed the site of the Jebusite city. The westward valley bears the infamous name *Vale of Gehenna*, where once stood the sacrificial altars to Moloch, a place so fearful as to be a synonym for hell.

The Golden Gate (*overleaf*) is the only blocked gate. This is the gate where, according to belief, the Jewish *Messiah* will enter the City, and through which Christ did enter. It was blocked by an apprehensive Sultan Suleiman (some say Saladin) for security reasons: legend claims that his motive was to ensure that no Jewish or Christian Messiah would enter his city. The pillars that support the Byzantine Gate are thought by some to be the gift of the Queen of Sheba to King Solomon.

This ancient olive tree (*overleaf*), in the Garden of Gethsemane facing the Golden Gate, stands with its seven sisters that perhaps witnessed Jesus setting out from here on his agonising road to the Cross. Its leaves have been plucked by pilgrims as a memento, for centuries.

|6

The Mount of Olives
(*upper background*)
is Judaism's most
revered burial ground.
For centuries, Jews were
brought here to be buried
close to the Valley of
Jehosophat, (Kidron)
where the Last Judgement
will take place. Jewish
pilgrims would stand on
these slopes to gaze
down on the Temple
Mount.

From above the Garden
of Gethsemane (*R*),
the Mount of Olives
descends into the Kidron
Valley, where, according
to ancient Jewish
belief, the trumpets of
universal resurrection
will sound and call forth
the righteous from their
graves.

9|10

Mount Zion is associated with the name of King David who is, according to legend, buried here *(L)*, where he stood when he decided to make Jerusalem his city. A symbolic tomb of David is preserved in the ancient synagogue on the top of the Mount. The *Last Supper*, Jesus' Passover meal with his disciples, took place, according to Christian belief, in an upper room of the synagogue.
Behind the synagogue stands the Dormition Abbey and Basilica served by the Benedictine Fathers.

The Mount of Olives *(R)* creates in the Christian mind perhaps the most vivid scenes of Jesus Christ's life. Here he wept for the fate of Jerusalem and suffered his Agony. Here he sat with his disciples and taught his students, and from here he ascended into heaven. The Basilica of the Agony in Gethsemane *(centre foreground)* is popularly called the Church of All Nations, to commemorate all those countries that contributed to its erection. Other churches commemorate Mary Magdalena and the Virgin Mary, who is believed to be buried here.

In the valley along the lower slopes of the Mount of Olives, with its ancient tombs, is the rock hewn tomb of Zacharius *(centre)* which hides a tunnel that leads into the pillared Bnei Hezir tombs, giving rise to the popular belief that the sons of Hezir, priests in the time of Herod, did not want to be separated from their forefathers.

Close by stands the impressive pillar, *(R)* by popular tradition named the *Tomb of Absalom*, and reviled as a memorial to the son of David who rebelled against his father. Experts agree that this one was only built 700 years after David.

13|14

The Tomb of Kings *(L)* to the north of the Old City, was thought to be the last resting place of the kings of Judah. In fact they belonged to the family of Queen Helena of Adiabene (54 B.C.E.), who converted to Judaism, and upon arriving in Jerusalem, dispatched emissaries to Egypt and Cyprus to bring food for the poor of the city. The good lady was also commended by the sages of the Talmud, for decorating the Temple with gold.

These steps *(R)*, more than 2000 years old, lead very possibly to the place where the Temple High Priest lived, in a house that gave him a magnificent view of the Temple Mount. The steps are popularly called the *Maccabean steps* after the Hasmonean family that expelled the Greeks from Jerusalem, and are believed to be from their time.

15|16

The livelihood and security of Jerusalem always depended on water sources which were outside the walls. To prevent enemy domination of vital water, the springs were concealed underground. Working with primitive tools and surveying instruments, King Hezekia's engineers excavated this water tunnel *(L)* from both ends (700 B.C.E.). Holding to an exact gradient of 1 in 250 all the way, then succeeded in joining both ends of the 582 yard long tunnel exactly as planned. Thereafter, the women of Jerusalem could draw their water at the *Pool of Siloam,* whence it came from the Gihon springs, without venturing outside the city walls.

Electricity and the telephone may have come to ancient Jerusalem but the Arabs in the Moslem Quarter still sit leisurely outside their cafes, sipping black coffee, smoking the *narghileh* (water pipe) and playing backgammon, as they have for hundreds of years *(R)*.

Jerusalem belongs to countless sects and orders of the Three Religions. Its streets and shrines are shared by all. The Armenian priest *(L)* in his traditional black robe and cowl is a representative of the first—now homeless—nation to embrace Christianity. His order lives in a *city within a city*—the Armenian Compound on Mount Zion, where they maintain a priceless museum and library and their own printing press. Here, in a city alleyway, he passes *yeshiva* boys of the Orthodox Ashkenazi Jewish community. The Orthodox Jew coming out of the Jaffa Gate *(centre)* is returning from prayer at the Western "Wailing" Wall. His traditional fur hat—the *shtreimel,* made of twelve pieces of fur for the twelve Tribes of Israel—proclaims that this is a Festival and he is a *Hasid,* follower of a great rabbi, and believer in mystical Judaism and the joy of life. The white robed Sisters of the *Pie Madri della Nigrizia* are coming from the Dormition Abbey on Mount Zion *(R),* where Christian tradition holds that Mary, mother of Jesus, lay in *eternal sleep.*

19|20|21

Armies and empires come and go. Scientists and engineers make great discoveries, but in Jerusalem, little changes. This Arab of Siloam still ploughs his plot, in the shade of the city wall, with a mule and ancient ploughshare *(L)*. On the other side of the city, by the Damascus Gate, his desert cousin transports his goods and himself on camelback undaunted by motor cars and traffic lights . . And little changes in the city markets *(overleaf)* The bazaars – vegetables, cloth, jewellery, perfumes etc. – cluster together each in its own street, with its wares hung prominently across the alleyway. Fashions may perhaps make some allowance for tourists, but Jerusalemites still use straw baskets and brooms and drink cold *sus* bought from the street vendor, and shafts of sunlight find their way through the arches.

The religious minded visitor has always been struck by the contrast between Jerusalem's metaphysical sanctity and its mundane life. The Arab village woman, wearing the traditional black gown and hand embroidered bodice, is crossing the corner of the great plaza where some Moslems believe, King Solomon sat every day to watch his workmen build the *Temple of the Lord (R)*. On the Via Dolorosa *(L)*, with its 2000 year old memories, life also goes on as usual.

▲ Citadel of David

Jerusalem is also a city of old people and old trades. The two venerable Jewish rabbis (*previous page*) are making their arduous way through the Dung Gate to pray at the Western Wall, and the Armenian grandmother passes the time of day in watching the crowds pouring through the city, with eyes that have seen it all before thousands of times. In the potter's yard, enthusiasts seek shards of centuries past, but the potter's wheel still turns, as it has for four millennia in Jerusalem, and the craftsmen are still adept at making "yesterday's" earthenware (*Left*).

Herod built three towers in his palace, the so-called Citadel of David on the slopes of Mount Zion, where by tradition David prayed to God and sang his *psalms of Israel*. When Titus destroyed the city (70 C.E.) he ordered these towers preserved as the defences of the Tenth Legion. The Moslem minaret and Crusader walls *(R)* rest on the foundations of the Tower of Phasael, named for Herod's brother. Following centuries of siege and battles, in which the Citadel always played a major role.

The two greatest scenes of Jewish pilgrimage are the Tomb of David and the Western Wall *(overleaf)*. Though crowds pour to the Western Wall every day, on Festivals it becomes the scene of mass pilgrimage and rejoicing. On the day of the *Rejoicing of the Law*, when the annual readings of portions of the Holy Book come to an end and world-wide Jewry begins again to read from the Book of Genesis *"in the beginning . . ."* congrega-tions of the city's synagogues bring their Scrolls of the Law in colourful processions to celebrate this happy day; close to Solomon's Temple.

The Western (*Wailing*) Wall is the only remnant of the outer walls of Herod's Temple, During the destruction (70 C.E.), all the efforts of Titus' legionnaires could not budge the great stones of this wall *(L)*. For more than nineteen hundred years, this wall has been closer to the hearts of Jews than any other shrine. It is the last remaining vestige of the great *Second Temple* that stood on Moriah, and Jews came here to weep over its destruction, and pray for redemption. In latter years, the Western Wall has become a symbol of *Zion reborn* and witnesses more joy than tears. Yet the legend of the *Wailing* Wall persists though another local legend attributes the popular name to the large tears of dew that roll down the face of the wall in the early hours of the morning.

The Orthodox don their prayer shawls and *tefilin* for it is written of God's Commandments *"and thou shalt bind them for a sign upon thine hand, and they shall be as frontlets between thine eyes."* (*Previous Page L*).

The crowns and ornamental cases (*previous page R*) are magnificent handworked silver and gold decorations from scrolls of the *Torah* placed on David's tomb in deference to and honour of the King.

The Messiah will come of the House of David. The ram's horn shofar is sounded to announce Festivals and to close them. It also has a traditional popular significance of opening the Gates of Heaven to prayer and of speeding the coming of the Messiah. So it is blown at the traditional tomb of David to awaken the slumbering king.

The great ancient and complex building in which the tomb is housed is holy to all three religions. Moslems revere it as the tomb of the Prophet David, and built a mosque over the synagogue. To Christians this is the place where the Last Supper was held.

*Never has the Divine Presence departed from the Western Wall.* So sayeth the Talmud, so prayers are offered up as close as possible, in the hope they will ascend through the crevices to the *Throne of Grace.* For centuries prayers and hopes written on small pieces of paper have been crammed into these crevices and the hallowed stones have been kissed by millions of believers *(L).*

The origins of the *lulav,* the myrtle, willow, citron and date palm, have been lost in antiquity *(R).* The Law of Moses and the Book of Nechemia command the collection of these four species for the building of the tabernacle on the annual Festival of *Succot,* but later interpretations have ascribed a symbolic meaning to each.

45|46

For a *barmitzvah* boy to read his Portion of the Law, that signifies his coming of age, by the Wall, is a great privilege to be remembered *(L)*.

*"For upon all the glory shall be a defence,"* so a canopy, the same as used for weddings, is carried over the Scroll of the Law, when this Sephardi community sets out from its synagogue to make the festive pilgrimage to the Western Wall *(R)*.

47|48

Jerusalem gives sanctuary to all the sects of the three religions. They exist one alongside the other. The Karaites believe only in the written Law of God and reject the Oral Law and the Talmud as being the work of man—and not of God. Their ancient underground synagogue (L) inside the Old City, dates back to the 8th century, when the sect was founded by Anan ben David.

Also underground, to the north of the city, the Tomb of the Judges was the burial place of members of Sanhedrin—the High Court of Israel, more than half of whom were executed when Herod ascended to his throne (37 B.C.E.). The tomb contains 71 burial niches hewn out of the natural rock.

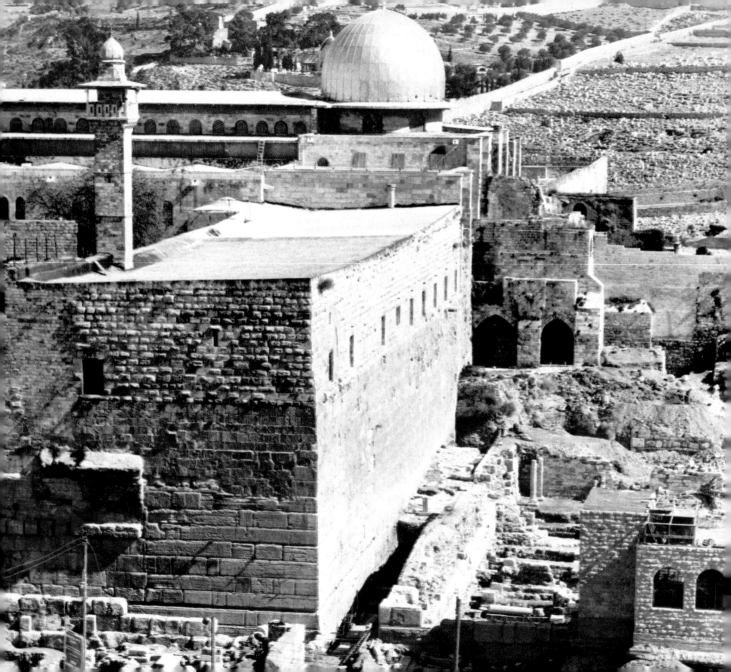

The desire and hope of uncovering and reconstructing the splendid past of Jerusalem during the period of the Second Temple has led archaeologists to excavate the south wall of the Mount, in the hope of reaching traces perhaps even of the entrance to Solomon's Temple *(L)*. Meanwhile they have unearthed this giant stone *(above)*—found on the Herodian pavement—believed to be from the south-west wall, where stood a tower from which a temple priest would announce the coming of the Sabbath by sounding a trumpet, the notes of which reverberated through the streets of the lower city. The Hebrew inscription reads *House of the Trumpet*. Other discoveries include the stone steps that connected the lower city with the Temple Mount and an ancient vessel marked *sacrifice* believed to be from the Inner Temple itself.

51|52

To the south of Jerusalem, lies the Tomb of Rachel, the beloved matriarch of popular Jewish tradition, and the only one not buried in Hebron, because she died on this spot giving birth to Benjamin. The tomb is venerated by Jews and Moslems and women come here to pray for fertility and successful childbirth. Within *(L)* and without *(R)* the building attests to the hands of Crusader, Moslem and Jewish builders.

כה אמר ה
מנעי קולך מבכי ועיניך מדמעה
כי יש שכר לפעלתך נאם ה
ושבו מארץ אויב

Wrapped in *talitoth* (prayer shawls), Jews stand in prayer before the Holy Ark. This synagogue is one of three beautiful Renaissance synagogues transported from Italy to Jerusalem in their entirety. The most ornate is from Conegliano near Venice and was originally built in the 15th century. Following the ancient tradition, the Scrolls of the *Torah* are kept in the *Holy Ark,* which elsewhere than in Jerusalem would always be on the wall of the synagogue which faces towards the Holy City.

Chagall's twelve great stained glass windows in the synagogue of the Hadassah Hospital, depict the twelve tribes of Israel. Each contains details traditionally associated with the particular tribe and a liberal sprinkling of the symbolic animals for which this Master is famous.
*(R).*

The Sabbath is ushered into Mea Shearim—*the quarter of the hundred gateways*—by a fanfare of youthful trumpets. The Sabbath Eve meal commences with the Blessing for Bread, performed over traditional *chalot*—plaited white loaves, to differentiate from the daily bread *(L)*.

Unlike other religions, the *rabbi* is by tradition teacher, interpreter and judge for his congregation rather than its secular leader. Students of the Law of Moses, young and old, have for centuries gathered at the feet of the great rabbis to study and interpret the *Torah,* and to question the rabbi— and sometimes dispute—over the interpretations by the *Sages of Israel,* contained in the vast tomes of the Talmud *(R)*.

Tradition has played a large part in
Jewish life since the destruction of the
Temple, and the traditions of hundreds
of years are not to be cast aside at the
will and whim of passing centuries.
Young boys of the Ashkenazi Orthodox community still begin their study
of the written and oral Law of God at
a very early age, and will continue
to immerse themselves in the Holy
Book through their first two decades
*(L)*. No less traditional is the laborious
and meticulous handwritten work of
the Bible Scribe, whose parchment
copies will be sewn into the scrolls used
in synagogues. He keeps his head
covered with the *talit*—prayer shawl—
because of the holiness of the writings.
His Yemenite colleague *(overleaf)* is a
silversmith, who lovingly completes the
ornate filigree decoration that will
adorn the outer case, perhaps of the
same scroll.

From time immemorial, the *shofar* has been the traditional means of announcing great portents. It is laboriously made from a perfect ram's horn, and fashioned to give the exact notes to open the Gates of Heaven to prayer offered during the Ten Days of Penitence, and to give notice of the end of the fast of the Day of Atonement, the most holy day in the Jewish religion.

61 | 62

The Law has been read from beginning to end; a new year is starting with Genesis and joy abounds. These white-shirted boys from a modern secular youth movement, spill out into the street for boisterous folk-dances, watched by a more sedate *hasid* in his silk coat and *shtreimel,* kept for festivals such as this. In another corner of the holy city, in front of *Hechal Shlomo,* the Chief Rabbinate, the *hakafot*—circling with the scrolls—also spills into the street, where all who desire the privilege can have their turn at dancing while holding the sacred *Torah* aloft.

Buying the four *species* of the *Lulav* for the Feast of Tabernacles is a careful business, for men only, for the slightest flaw would detract from their symbolic characteristics—analogies of man's life: the citron has taste and smell; the date has taste but no smell; the myrtle has smell but no taste; and the willow possesses neither—all are of the earth and sun.

65|66

Mea Shearim—*the hundred gateways*—built a hundred years ago was among the first quarters erected outside the city walls. It has changed little since. Its houses, somewhat reminiscent of the ghettos of Eastern Europe, were built close together in narrow lanes for better protection against marauders. Its men still dress in traditional black coats, summer and winter alike, and wear long beards and ear-locks, often tucked back over their ears; women dress modestly and their traditional hair-pieces—*sheitel*—are concealed beneath shawls and scarves to prevent their attracting men other than their husbands, as the Law of Moses commands. Public notices, repeated at intervals throughout the quarter, warn visitors to respect the modesty of dress as practised in the quarter (previous page *R*). 67|68

The prayer to the full moon is recited under the open sky, and is therefore posted outside the synagogue in giant letters, decipherable in the moonlight, which has contributed to the Hebrew idiom: *letters of moon sanctification*—implying words so clear that one cannot but see them *(L)*.

A man of Mea Shearim hastens through the narrow picturesque alleyways of the quarter, to take part in daily prayers.

The origins of the *Memouna Festival (overleaf)* celebrated by the North African Jewish community—who flock to Jerusalem for the occasion, dressed in their traditional *berber* gowns—are shrouded in mystery. It is doubtful whether the participants themselves know the traditional reasons but what does it matter—a good time is had by all, and the traditional food, drink and dances are for them the event of the year.

69|70

The City of David on the *Ophel* to the south of Mount Moriah, is part of a 1:50 reproduction of the Old City as it was in 66 C.E., built on a carefully and accurately contoured slope in the western city. Under the meticulous supervision of a leading archaeologist Prof. Avi-Yonah artisans, students and artists laboured for years to construct the scale model of Jerusalem of Herod the Great in miniature, bringing to life the full glory of the past, and using the original materials from which the buildings were built.

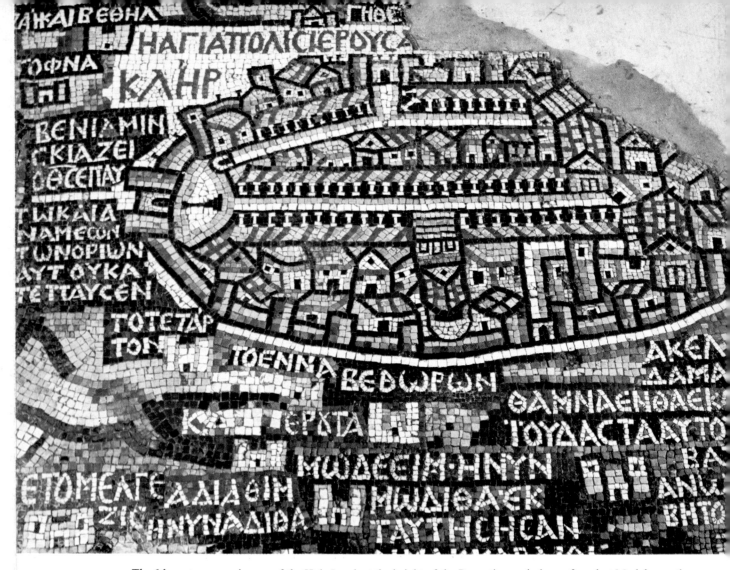

The 6th century mosaic map of the Holy Land, at the height of the Byzantine period, was found at Madeba on the Dead Sea in 1897. Its perspective view of Jerusalem is the oldest existent representation of the city, and some of its detail, inscribed in Greek, has been confirmed by archaeological excavations.

Inside pages—Jerusalem panoramic view from Mount of Olives. *Left* skyline—Mount Zion. *Right Foreground*—Dominus Flevit.

Standing on a hill overlooking the edge of the Wall is the *Rockefeller*-Palestine Archaeological Museum—spreading over ten acres and thousands of years of magnificent exhibits, from pre-historic Carmel man and bas-reliefs from the palace of Sennacherib at Nineveh, to precious architectural details from the Holy Sepulchre Church and the Al Aksa Mosque.

Centrepiece of the Old City model at the *Holyland Hotel,* is the Inner Temple, *the holy of holies* of the Second Temple, reproduced in its original marble according to all the details known from ancient documents.

Panorama of the Holy City from a window in the *Dominus Flevit* which marks the site from which Jesus looked on the Temple Mount and the city and prophesied its destruction according to the Gospels: *"and when he was come near, he beheld the city, and wept over it"*. The chapel roof is tear-shaped.

The Franciscan
Fathers,
representatives of
the *Holy See*
responsible for the
shrines of their
church in the Holy
Land, come every
Friday afternoon
to re-enact the
*Way of the Cross*,
starting from the
first station and
ending at the Holy
Sepulchre Church.
The Ist Station
of the Cross by
tradition
commemorates
the place where
Jesus was
condemned to
death. It is a
courtyard of the
*Al-Omaria* school
facing the Convent
of the Sisters of
Zion, where stood
the Antonia
Fortress,
traditionally the
place where Jesus
was sentenced by
Pontius Pilate to
death on the cross.

Known as the *Ecce homo* (here is the man), this arch traditionally marks the place where Pilate brought Jesus out to the people. The arch itself was built by Hadrian. Towering over it are the Chapel of Condemnation and its neighbour— the Chapel of the Flagellation.

Coming up the Via Dolorosa, clearly marked for all comers *(L)* as the *Street of the Sorrows*, is the IIIrd Station where Jesus first stumbled under the weight of the Cross. For centuries this spot was marked by a simple pillar, which is now a corner-post in the fence of the Polish Chapel built in 1947.

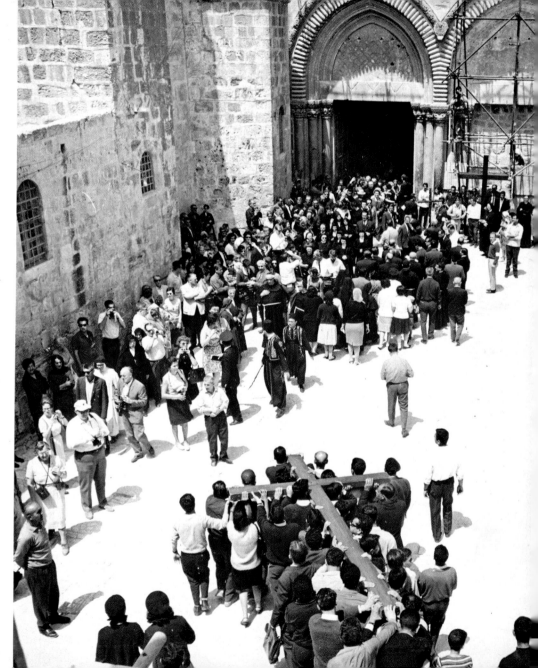

Most sacred of all Christian shrines in the Holy Land, the Church of the Holy Sepulchre was first built by the Byzantine Emperor Constantine in the 4th century. Within its walls are Stations X to XIV of the Cross where Jesus was stripped, nailed to the Cross, died, was taken down and laid to rest on Calvary Hill. For long centuries, by order of Saladin, Christians were permitted the use of the church, for so long as the key remained in Moslem hands. Devout Christian pilgrims bear the Cross past all the Stations of the Via Dolorosa, and into the Holy Sepulchre in solemn procession.

"*For the Angel of the Lord descended from heaven, and came and rolled back the stone from the door, and sat upon it.*" The stone, symbol of that rolled back from the door, upon which Gabriel sat, stands in the entrance to the traditional tomb of Jesus. Facing this doorway is the *navel of the world*, a Crusader urn which, according to legend, marks the centre of the earth.

Devout of all denominations and from all continents, join the procession up the Via Dolorosa, past the Stations of the Cross, on Good Friday morning *(L)*. Pilgrimage to Jerusalem has always been of great significance to Christians, despite all obstacles and difficulties.

*"Now in the place where he was crucified, there was a garden"*. Many Christians and especially the Protestant denominations believe the Garden Tomb, just outside the northern wall of the city, to be *Golgotha*—the burial place that belonged to Joseph of Arimathea, from which Jesus rose to Heaven.

The Upper Chamber on Mount Zion commemorates the place where Jesus' last Passover —the *Last Supper* —was held with his disciples around him *(L)*. Starting from another mountain— the Mount of Olives— the Palm Sunday procession of all Christian denominations and ages, sings *Hossana* and bear palm branches to commemorate Jesus' triumphant entry into Jerusalem. These convent school children *(R)* will enter the city past the Church of St. Anne as the Golden Gate is blocked.

The Armenians were the first nation to accept Christianity. Their spiritual centre in the Cathedral of St. James, *(R & L)* holds magnificent art and treasures of the Armenian patriarchate. Its walls are covered with antique tiles and its floors with rich oriental carpets. These treasures have accumulated over fifteen hundred years of residence of the Armenian community in Jerusalem.

The many Eastern churches add much colour and Oriental atmosphere to Jerusalem's religious ritual. The Ethiopians here in their Easter Sunday procession trace their origins back to the Queen of Sheba who visited Solomon in Jerusalem, and the entrance to their church is decorated with a relief of the *Lion of Judah*, traditional symbol of the royal dynasty of Ethiopia. Their banners carried on festivals are decorated in a traditional and typical manner.

The Greek Orthodox ceremony of the Washing of the Feet *(R)* is a traditional sign of humility that has found its place in every Christian denomination. The patriarch casts aside his fine raiment and washes the feet of his priests and followers as did Jesus at the Last Supper.

Outside the city walls on the site of Herod's stone quarry, from which the giant pillars were apparently cut for the Temple, stands the Russian Orthodox Church *(overleaf)*, in architecture typical of the Slav Orthodox churches.

This mosque—the Al Aksa—is the third holiest shrine in Islam, after Mecca and Medina, and has always drawn the faithful—mystics and dervishes, priests and students—to drink of its inspiration.

"*Glorified be he who carried His servant by night from the Inviolable Place of Worship to the Far Distant Place of Worship.*" The great inscription worked in ceramic around the Dome of the Rock, is from the Koran's Mecca Revelation—*the Children of Israel*—which relates the Prophet's vision of being carried by night on the Heavenly Steed, from Mecca to Jerusalem, from whence he ascended through the seven heavens to the presence of God, to receive injunctions on the prayers of the faithful *(L)*.

Faithful Moslems pass the great Dome on their way from Friday prayer, across the wide Moriah Plaza from the Dome.

*"Oh ye who believe! When you rise up for prayer . . . Wash your feet up to the ankles."* The *El-Kas* where the faithful are commanded to wash their feet before prayer, draws its water from one of the thirty-four water holes on Mount Moriah. From the *El-Kas,* Moslems proceed to the Al Aksa, leaving their shoes and sandals in orderly lines by the great doorway and entering barefoot.

96|97

The interior of the Al Aksa built in the 7th century, showing the fine pillars, arches and roofing. On Fridays of each week, thousands of Moslems sit, cross-legged, line by line, facing Mecca on the beautiful Oriental carpets that cover the floor of the Al Aksa. Others of the faithful of Islam kneel on their prayer rugs in the Plaza between the Al Aksa and the Dome of the Rock, in orderly lines which are perhaps more illustrative of the disciplined brotherhood of Islam than any other phenomenon. The women remain separate and veiled, in the name of modesty as the Koran commands (*overleaf*). Friday prayer for them becomes a day to meet friends and relatives.

So magnificent is the Dome of the Rock, first built by the Khalif Omar, with its many coloured marble, ceramics, enamelled woodwork, typical of the best in Islamic architecture, that the Crusaders believed it to be the fabled *Second Temple*. The so-called *Mosque of Omar* is in fact not a mosque at all but a dome erected over the sacred rock (*overleaf*), where legend claims that Abraham offered up Isaac in sacrifice, and from whence Muhammad ascended to heaven on *Al-Burak*—the heavenly steed. Legend attributes the indentations on the Rock to the footprints of Abraham and Muhammad, and in the cave below to the fingers of the archangel Gabriel as he clawed his way up the rock to escort Muhammad on his night ascent.

The Kiss of
kinship
when
relatives
meet for
Friday
prayer and
the faithful
kneeling
towards
Mecca when
the Muezzin
calls to
prayer *(R)*.

A stone's throw away and a seeming world apart, modern Jerusalem *(L)* with its population of almost a quarter of a million Jews, Moslems and Christians is a bustling administrative, secular and lay centre—forever building and changing, yet always pervaded by the atmosphere and consciousness of the *Eternal City*. Its modern buildings and squares—like Paris Square *(above)*—glow at sundown with the same golden glow that lights the stones of the city walls.

106|107

אושוויץ-אוסווינצ'ים
AUSCHWITZ-OSWI

מיידאנק
MAJDANEK

The pathways leading to the *Yad Vashem* monument to the six million Jewish dead of Nazi Europe, are lined with the trees of the *Avenue of the Righteous*, each named for a Gentile who risked his life to save Jews from the *Holocaust*. The simple and stark interior of the monument lists the infamous death camps, under the light of the *everlasting flame*.

The *Onion dome* of the Hebrew University synagogue stands out against the skyline of the suburb of Bet Hakerem
—*House of the Vineyard*. Within the dome the synagogue floor appears to float in space, giving an ethereal effect
most appropriate to a house of prayer.

Picnics have become a popular way of celebrating Independence Day in Jerusalem ▶

The coming of Festivals and great events was announced by the lighting of beacons on Mount Scopus, hence its name. The Sages of Israel commanded that he who sees Jerusalem from Scopus must rent his clothes in mourning for the Temple. The Jewish People dreamt for centuries of the Jewish University in the Holy Land. The dream reached fulfillment when the cornerstone of the Hebrew University was laid—on Mount Scopus in 1918.

Students in a social
debate (*Previous
Page R*) in a
night-club and on
the second campus
at Givat Ram *(R)*.

The Givat Ram campus of the Hebrew University was only begun in 1954. In keeping with the commandment *"Thou shalt not make unto thee any graven image,"* the campus is remarkably free of any sculpture. The magnificent *Reclining Woman* by Henry Moore is a rare and outstanding exception.

The impressive bronze candelabra that stands in the square before Israel's Parliament—the *Knesset*—is the work of Benno Elkan *(R)*. It was a gift to the Knesset from the House of Commons in London. The seven-branched candelabra is the symbol of state of Israel, following the tradition of the candelabra that stood in the Second Temple; the inspiration for this one came from the frieze on *Titus' Arch* in Rome, which shows slaves carrying away the candelabra from the Temple in Jerusalem.

The bronze panels are devoted to remarkably sensitive reproduction of scenes in Jewish history through four millenia. In the top centre panel Aaron and Hur support Moses' arms for *"and it came to pass when Moses held up his hand, that Israel prevailed: and when he let down his hand, Amalek prevailed."* The panel below is devoted to the stone tablets engraved with the *Ten Commandments,* given by God to Moses on Mount Sinai.

In the horseshoe-shaped Knesset (*right*), any member wishing to speak comes to the podium. The long table in the centre is the *Government bench.*

Across the valley from the Knesset *(L background)*, stands the Shrine of the Book *(foreground)*, permanent repository of the *Dead Sea Scrolls* and the *Nahal Hever Letters*. The entrance is down a long tunnel, designed to give the feeling of entering an underground cave, like the Qumran Caves where the Scrolls were discovered. Below the Israel Museum *(R background)*, of which the Shrine of the Book is a part, stands the Greek Orthodox Monastery of the Cross *(above)* in the valley of the Cross, on the spot where, by tradition, stood the tree from which the Cross was fashioned.

Under the dome, shaped to resemble the lids of the jars in which the scrolls lay for centuries, the *Book of Isaiah* enjoys pride of place in the exhibits of the Shrine of the Book. Although for centuries the Bible was handed down by word of mouth, this scroll, the only complete one, confirms that the oral version was true to the original in every last detail. It is perhaps appropriate that the Book of Isaiah *(close-up, R)*, the *Desert Prophet*, should have been preserved in a desert cave, where the Qumran sect kept its holy books.

Alongside the Dead Sea
Scrolls (*overleaf*) and the
Bar Kochba letters, the
modular structures of the
Israel Museum house a rich
collection of Jewish folklore
and religious articles—and
a fine archaeological exhibit,
representative of all periods
in the history of the Holy
Land *(overleaf R)*. The wide
gravel *platform*, landscaped
by a Japanese master, makes
an impressive setting for the
Billy Rose Sculpture Garden
that surrounds the Museum.
Its great collection,
encompassing old and
modern masters, includes
works by Rodin, Moore,
Daumier, Epstein and
Picasso *(following pages)*.

Canaanite gate from the
Kingdom of Hazor (pre-
Israelite) *(p. 125)*.
"The Diabolo player" by
Germaine Richier *(p.126)*.

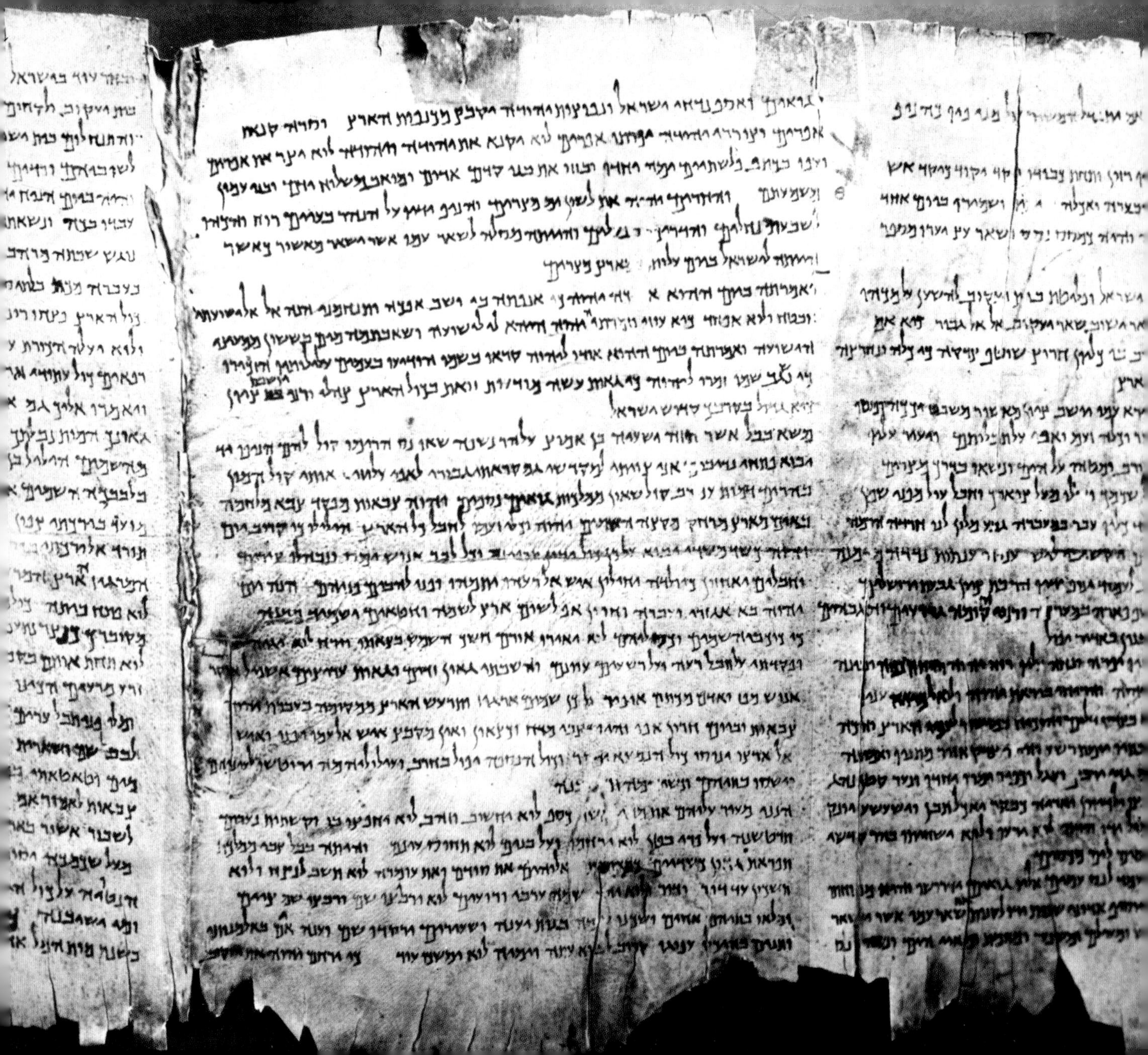

The three thousand seat
National Congress Hall
gives Jerusalemites the
opportunity of hearing
frequent orchestral concerts
in congenial surroundings
and good acoustics. *(L)*.

On a forested hilltop to the
west of Jerusalem stands
a memorial to John F.
Kennedy, President of the
United States *(R)*. The
monument, reminiscent of
a great tree cut in its prime,
is formed of ribs, each
representing a State of the
Union and adorned with
its crest.

128|129

The *Yemin Moshe quarter,* facing Mount Zion, was built outside the city wall by Sir Moses Montefiore in 1860. Above the quarter, he ordered erection of a windmill to provide a livelihood for the inhabitants. The windmill is now a museum devoted to Montefiore and his great works in the Holy Land, and the quarter is now a flourishing artists' colony. The flourishing colony and the ancient—still green—olive trees best symbolise the roots of continuing life in Jerusalem and its obstinate grasp on history and men's hearts.

Photo Credits

Amit Itzhak. Studio Garo. Lieber Menachem. Perlmuter David.
Toren Avraham and Israel Press Division.